PARAM

FIRST POETS 8

 Canada Council
for the Arts

Conseil des Arts
du Canada

 ONTARIO ARTS COUNCIL
CONSEIL DES ARTS DE L'ONTARIO

Guernica Editions Inc. acknowledges the support of the Canada Council
for the Arts and the Ontario Arts Council.
The Ontario Arts Council is an agency of the Government of Ontario.

SUZANNE ROBERTSON

PARAMITA, LITTLE BLACK

GUERNICA

TORONTO – BUFFALO – LANCASTER (U.K.)

2011

Elana Wolff, editor
Guernica Editions Inc.
P.O. Box 117, Station P, Toronto (ON), Canada M5S 2S6
2250 Military Road, Tonawanda, N.Y. 14150-6000 U.S.A.

Distributors:
University of Toronto Press Distribution,
5201 Dufferin Street, Toronto (ON), Canada M3H 5T8
Gazelle Book Services, White Cross Mills, High Town, Lancaster LA1 4XS U.K.

First edition.
Printed in Canada.

Legal Deposit – First Quarter
Library of Congress Catalog Card Number: 2010939642
Library and Archives Canada Cataloguing in Publication
Robertson, Suzanne, 1974-
Paramita, little black / Suzanne Robertson.
(First poets series ; 8)
ISBN 978-1-55071-336-7
I. Title. II. Series: First poets series (Toronto, Ont.) ; 8
PS8635.O2289P37 2011   C811'.6   C2010-906769-X

Contents

For my parents,
and for Stephanie
and Rosemary

To the Point

To the man who listened to the sun as if it were
an orator along the path to freedom
To the long saga of his beard that began
in the Middle East

      To the open door of the lake

To the sailboats moving like brides towards the altar
    of blue
To the rollerblader who wants to party like it's 1999
To the trees practicing Tai Chi
in the wind

To the constellations of black flies
To the sea gulls in Salvation Army suits above the
    Gardiner

      To their mental cries

To the tigers growling beneath the hoods of cars
To the dogs jonesin' at the end of leashes

To the woman who was afraid to take me by the
    hand
To the men who were breathing at our backs
To the sky that did not let down its fire
                    escape
To the city that keeps us from touching
each other

            To the point
where it crumbles

To the rocks that appear kinder
than most
To their hospitality hosting
                                    the view
To the geese walking like grandparents
along the beach

To the boy who took out his chopsticks and
        serenaded
the night on a xylophone of stars

Sibling of the Air

She's packed her thread and needle,
her watercolours, flip-flops, flashlight, her big
toes, her credo.

She's packed the lipstick of autumn, and the river's
tin drum tympanum.

She's packed her Chatwin, her phrasebook, her
    parents
circa 1974, her sister the eraser, that small pink
nipple on the pencil.

* * *

From the lounge window I see the eyes
of the cockpit alight.
The pilot removes his hat, ears bud boyish
and irreverent from this man I must trust
with my twin-engine heart, my lowbrow
fandango, my mineral-spirits talk,
my rainy-day mojo.

* * *

I stared at her eyes bent like horseshoes
over goodbye and good luck,
watched her pass through metal

gates blowing see-ya-kid
kisses, until I waved her on and pocketed
my open-faced palm.
She turned,
lowered her hand to half-mast,
shifted a life from shoulder to shoulder,
took on the identity of someone
who knows exactly
where she's going.

With one ticket and the soft currency
of her western hair,
she wants to be lost in a new hemisphere,
to hear the monsoon
lungs of the rain or the sun stepping out to say:

    here is a cloud is a shadow to welcome
    to lay down your keys,
    your watch,
    the tired knees
    of every bad thought,
    because tomorrow died peacefully
    in her sleep,
    and yesterday doled out
    second chances, gathered
    your family around the oak table,
    and everyone wore apologies
    on their faces,
    and laughed so hard
    in the deepwooded heart
    of today, day, day.

* * *

Once the plane has taken off
I'll find a phone,
tell Dad his eldest has made
a sibling of the air.

* * *

Manmade thunder and torn open
stare, alone
with her departure's tiny
bone in my throat, not even a jetstream

to Hanoi to Vientiane to Phnom Penh to Bangkok to
    Mandalay

Against the window
a bowed head,
holding steadfast to the earth, and taken
from the asylum of the one
who has fled.

Fear of Death Confounds Me

I've spent the day reading poems written in 1986.
They're about a woman's love affair with the world.
It began for a girl in a one-room school with the
plainspoken verse that came down from the clouds
and told her things. Simple, noble things. The way
she outlined every object: the perennial, the pear,
the bed, the bat, the wind in the arms of a shirt. Each
day the white cells of winter stacking up against
her, covering the bone meal in the garden. Some
days the animal pressed against her leg and happi-
ness stared in the window, pointed to a vase of
flowers. Elbows carried the delicate heads of new-
borns, hearts were stranded in their lifeboats, mar-
riages were ditched in middle age, though not hers.
The past grinds a thick lens from memory, tricks us
into looking back: the way longing hangs like a
woman's stocking in the shower, it leads to the
medicine cabinet filled with multi-coloured pills,
thoughts of not continuing.

In 1986 my love affair began. Parents irrevocably
split like the wedges of fruit they fed to children. A
dog was left in a wooden house to drink the frozen
pond in his water bowl, find the circumference of
life at the end of a chain. Children slept side by side
in the hallway like vibrations of light. They knew
how to meet halfway, lie down on a bed of compro-
mise. Surrounded by wallflowers, afghans, ceramic
nightlights, all the lonely mother-hobbies. Children

travelled between adults like messages in a bottle. Father-houses had to understand nightmares, back-rubs, the satellites of small ears recording everything, how to build a room of sorry. I've spent the day reading poems written in 1986. They have entered the marrow of me, travelled through a catheter in time. Even though I know the world is always splitting and its breaking is where I continue to go, *timor mortis conturbat me*. And where does this leave us, besides here: wanting to go where the last door leads us.

Take Notes

The secretary wonders why the first one goes
Down faster than a glass of water why

The dandy hours have her disappearing
In side view mirrors still pedaling

But with insincerity in her legs

Pace yourself aging girl who's been left
In the ditch of her thirties –

What did Virginia say?

* * *

Where is all this failure supposed to go?
She wonders and gives the moon

A salute from her plastic chair that keeps watch over

The good Samaritans as they move
Like tragedies in the wind

Red and yellow petals pirouette and embark
Like knights from the round table

She hears the rustle of two cats falling
In love

Their bodies carpet the grass
And the shape of desire is painful
But the dog is there to say *breathe in the crushed*
Dampness so she touches his small dark

Forehead to bring the cave-like nature of her mind

Back home

* * *

Her eyelids have lost their tension and rest
Like cheapskate blinds

Volume Three of *These Days*
Plays on

She cranks up the stainless steel knob of the
     universe
And sits at her desk like Captain Kirk

Staring out the window at an enterprise of grey
Beam me up beam me up, she says to her loss

Of faith and uses some masking tape
To hold normal together

* * *

Yellow-label Australian and evening
In the throat chardonnay

With greens abiding the terrible scent
Of sadness rising up from the lawn

* * *

Today she saw a White Coat

Who talked about recovery

As a mountain you never stop climbing

Always the hanging valleys

Pitfalls and jingle-jangle

Parables to gag on

Then she went to the bar and sat with Jesus

Who tried his best to come
Down from the cross but couldn't

So she went home and baked

A cake that was called

In Love with Daylight

* * *

It's strange times on the shortwave Wednesday
   morning

She wants to enjoy the last explosion of sobriety
Before her serotonins start their trapeze act

She's afraid of lists alphabets and FIGARO

FIGARO FIGARO

Orange flowers holding their Cirque du Soleil faces
Up to the window

She turns to the mirror's perfect circle
Closes her eyes and roars an operatic tongue

Rolls out the red carpet

But the satchel of sound remains
Caught in her throat

* * *

She will try not to fall asleep at work today
Her shoulders move like sting-rays above the
   keyboard

In the filing room she hears her mother's *gentle-
   gentle*

17

Pats the top of her head until she drifts

Into the silent pasture of no recall
The computer screen blank-faces her

Like a bored security guard And high heels ice pick
    the marble

Waiting rooms of appointments
On her coffee break she sits on a bench

And ransacks her conversations
Like a spy checking a room for wiretaps

* * *

Outside Noodle Hut
A man speaks French beside her nice

Habitable park-bench-sound
Fleurs he says and the Seine flows by

She looks around the food court
Puts the river aside and writes:

    Anyone with handbags

    Anyone with doubts and addresses

    Anyone who has lost their specificity

Dr. Sullivan has eyes like the centre

Of a blueberry pie

Crushed and old-fashioned

Ruddy hair styled like the waves

Children draw on a blackboard

Forty-something wrinkles

Blue short sleeves

Pale arms stronger than a code of ethics

Blue tie

Blue buttons

Blue breast pocket

Blue-lidded pen standing like the UN soldier in
Bujumbura

Who waved to her every morning from the
watchtower

Blue pants

Blue veins

Freckled hands that are the opposite

Of lies

                    * * *

To the mirror she waves:

   Hello there Crumplestiltskin

Locks the door

                    * * *

The secretary picks up the bottle of pills
And stares at herself

   Anyone with a lion caught in their face

Her hands begin to have a nervous breakdown
They flicker like old chandeliers in haunted houses
She has on her professional blouse
Places her nose in the fabric

It smells of ink and the faint parental scent of wood

The pills are small mighty vessels half-blue
Half-white light as fingernails
She swallows them with a strange cocktail of
   resignation

And disbelief

Strange anthem of raw experience sticking its
   needles
Into her chakras

Somewhere a man with hair like the Rings of Saturn
Scratches his head and remembers the woman
Doing laundry in the basement

She calls her mother to hear the domestics

Maybe the Popeye-spit
Of bacon in the fry pan

The dishwasher having a fit in the corner
Oven doors opening with jaws of sensibility

All the bottles in the cold storage room
Waiting like wild horses in the dark

* * *

At the corner of Kennedy & Eglinton if she turned

To the left she could enter the river
Of transports trucks buses sedans and jalopies
   taking
The innocent cargo across the finish line

She could end her census on beauty
And muzzle the hound of love
That yaps to no one in the backyard of her thoughts
    Anyone with reasons on their lips

If she turned to the right she could see the white
Hijab touching the child's cheeks with angelic
Self-defeat

* * *

What did Virginia say?

* * *

Tuesday morning with a violinist water-skiing
That bow across the horizon there is a strong-armed
    sunrise

Up ahead and leaves moving like fingers in the
    ragtime wind
If someone was here she would slap their shoulder
    for no good

Reason the bow keeps striking her
Not with optimism but a simple dose of maybe

Which is better than the two-timing
Fiddler called hope

* * *

and the pain goes

The Prescription

The hardworking length of a floorboard

The dog's belly-flop after bark! bark! bark! hangs

Like yellow ribbons in the tree

The gummy horselaugh hidden

Beneath the upper lip

The waves that shoulder the weighty ride to ruin

The thumbprint of enough on the eardrum

Of goodnight thinking maybe she should conjure
the barbwire

Crown of forgiveness

Thinking the colour green could make a fortune

Leaves all bursting with potential

Trees with their soft rock gazes

Birds showing her the exodus

Clouds comforting the brainstem

And beauty there finding a vein

Asking the secretary

To swing from it

Flying

I look around at the passengers, a mixture of folks
    and lawyers
all heading to Winnipeg on a Wednesday night. A
    young girl
offers me the seat beside her, palms open, fluttering.
Language left back on earth.

We're all immigrants this close to heaven.

Evening arrives through the window. The woman
    ahead of me
doesn't look up from her crossword, doesn't notice
    the sun
setting fire to her brown hair. Aisles are lined with
leather shoes, old sneakers, exposed ankles and
    briefcases.
This is all I know of the other passengers: some have
    nervous
feet that pace like animals beneath their seats, some
    order
drinks with loud, inflated voices, some face the wall
and cry into dinner napkins.

Now the young girl's head drops. Her body moves
like a marionette, stringed to the machinery of sleep.
    Eyes
half-closed, dreaming, not dreaming. Then she
    bends
to find her detachable hood, places her face inside

and finds night.
We are all flying to Winnipeg.

We might've loved each other,
had we ever met.

Rosemary

At ninety-nine she has survived the Great
Depression, two world wars, and fifty years of
    Protestant
propriety with a Catholic girl's inner rosary
and the wrung-out wrists of domestic
husbandry. In the end she was lifting a man
twice her size to the bathroom. When he died
the apartment quieted, long hours were washed
away with a mix of sorrow and bleach,
eventually the blue chair's empty seat could hold
her grief. In the mornings she began waking up to
    hind-
sight and her single life: breakfast with Jerry
Springer, swearing because it pleased her, midnight
    baths
with a good romance, finding the middle of the bed,
keeping her ulcer well fed, eating peaches from a tin
can, a shot of apricot brandy and God-talk at
    three a.m.

Goodness

You were raised in small town Ontario,
filled with streets too wide to beg upon,
car lots, strip malls, swollen

rivers and the melodramatic
repose of willow trees that shame
you with a desire
for endings. Always on the outskirts,
rooted at the edge of things: water, streets,
conversations. Taking pages
of useless notes:

Roxana grabs my arm as if
it were a railing. We enter the interview
room together and she shakes

in front of the immigration
officer, pronouncing all the Persian
G's in English, as in

I did nothing-g wrong-g.

* * *

Today a woman enters a restaurant
in Jerusalem and opens her coat.
Today the bright explosion

of sun hits your face
when you walk past a girl in
her underwear at the corner

of Queen and Sherbourne, hands
on her hips like a gunslinger,
knuckles studded with blood.

Today you drive past
the pruned horizon of apple orchards,
noticing the early winter
snow that saddles the backs of horses,
and your mother avoids the night
surgeon by organizing her pill

cupboard at 4 a.m.
as she waits for dawn to lie down
on a gurney of sleep.

* * *

Roxana and I walk Yonge Street.
It is too hard to trust anyone,
no? she asks

(sometimes, yes)

and chain-links our elbows,
describes her life before
and after the revolution.

Outside a crowded café,
I notice the dark comma inside
everyone's ears.

I grew up in a city outside
Tehran, we all lived
under one roof. She pauses,

lowers her voice, Sometimes I think I go
crazy missing-g them. My mother maybe
dying-g in that place.

* * *

You watch the evening news, see a woman
trampled into the red-dirt road of another
country. And you

      can't turn away
until the camera does, when the traffic
of feet across her body is replaced

by a weatherman creating small,
entropic swirls with his hands, pushing
blizzards across a map

      of North America.
And then your friend on Rogers Road
makes headlines when her father shoots

her mother in the kitchen, then turns
the gun on himself. Their modest
brick bungalow sold, new children

on the doorstep,
in the windows the faces of bystanders,
dried flower beds that have lost

the seeds of their eyes. When you
return home she is still there
behind the deli counter,

slicing cold cuts,
Black forest or smoked meat?
Her voice a nervous blade

of grass, as you stare down the strange,
lonely corridor of small talk.
Goodness me, she would say,

it has been too long,
and hands over the soft package of meat,
wrought with violence.

* * *

For you there are only words that amount
to nothing more than breathy pauses,
broken English and arm in arm

attempts to brace

yourself for the arrow of a crooked
ankle that leads to a delicate foot

lying on a street corner. Because everyday
you are pierced with either looking
or trying not to. Because

       there is a difference
between yearning for what you want
and wanting what the world

withholds. Because goodness asks
too much, but you don't know how
to give up on its empty-handed
       offerings, or roots
by the river that will one day
drag the veins of you.

Because upon fleeing Iran,
Roxana left behind her family,
her lover, and her breast.

       For a long time
I was angry, I even stopped
praying-g and then the cancer

meta… meta…
       (metastasized?)

Yes, it burned through me.
I lost everything-g,
even my eyes,

I mean my hair,
my eyebrows and yet
I lived, but these parts of me

are still missing-g. And she runs
her finger down the silicone
valley of her chest.

Because your mother's
prosthesis hides like an accomplice
inside her closet.

Because the women you love are taken
away piece by piece. And odds say
your time is coming.

And he will bring mortal
instruments. But don't be afraid. Others
have lain down whole and risen

to tell fragments
of the same story.

The Move

I came over and we twisted open the mouths
of bottles. You shoved clothes into garbage bags
with a softly bitten lower lip. Lilies in the backyard
went their separate ways, so you tied a piece
of string around them. To keep them together;
a piece of string. The staircase finally realized
what was going on and released your hand.
The lamps were stark naked
and the laundry room was better off
in the dark. We dismantled the bed like those
    shipwreckers
in Chittagong and you began jumping up and down
to keep from crying. There was a bottle
within reaching distance for ten hours straight,
smoke breaks, long hauls from the tailpipe. Many
    times
I couldn't explain what I was feeling –
when we sat on the kitchen floor and your shoulders
lay down their burden, lost in the silence
of the colander.
       At 1 a.m. we knocked
ourselves out with the last dregs of nonsense
and truth. I'm thinking about the post-Betty Ford
sunglasses with the safety pin keeping the arms on,
ex-heirlooms, cut crystal safe as children
in cardboard boxes, endings that require signatures.
When we climbed the stairs to your bedroom
the freedom of the mattress reminded me
of Sexton, it felt honest as straw beneath my body.

In the morning the movers appeared Herculean
and claustrophobic in your hallway. I shared
    a Black Oak
with a man whose face was the tip of an ice berg.
Then they threw their arms around everything
we couldn't carry.

A Conversation with Horizon

Turn to me.

I always do.

Tell me something.

Why do I break
my teeth on you?

Why are you standing there staring?

There's no room
to inch a word in
edgewise.

I don't understand.

The bar is aglow
with brighter voices.
I'm lock-jawed,
a tooth grinder behind
an earnest mouth,
a nightlong hesitation,
a silence bender.

Oh?

The booze makes me
a hound around conversations.

My tongue tends to
lollygag on the lip
too long.

What do you really want?

To stand in this corner
alone, watch you ink
the grey with the pen-tip
of night.

That sounds very quiet.

Sometimes it's enough
to hang your ear
on the eavestrough
of small talk,
to notice
the last cashew
that smiles
in the bowl,
the man
at the bar,
olive-eyed
with martinis.

Is laughter a way in?

Or out.
There are rules:
laugh but don't laugh
like a dilettante,
laugh like you're in on it,

like there's nothing
left to lose,
laugh like Baraheni.

Who's that?

A writer.

Where is he from?

Against a prison wall
Baraheni found the window
to his Caspian blue,
middle moon,
the mothertongue
his mother
never knew.

So it's the story you're after.

Every now
and then it climbs
into a canoe
and paddles towards me.

Slowly.

One stroke at a time.

Meanwhile the world surges on.

Meanwhile
I drag my heels on

a moment that
glistens like the waiter's
upper lip, dealing
coasters from
his blackjack, girl-wrists.
The way cheers

resound like a bell
in the town square
of our chests,
and we eye-to-eye
each other for luck,
feel struck
by that clash of irises.

It's about time, the intervals, nostalgia.

No. I've given up
on nostalgia,
pour it back
down that
bottomless well.
I prefer Baraheni's
broken verse,
all the places his mind
flew, handwriting
a path up the wall
to find his Zagros
mountain-view.

What are you sad about?

What if someone
is listening?
            Everyone's listening.

Shhh. I hear a woman
chasing a theory
between the trees
to explain exactly
where the girl was lost.

            You can begin anywhere.

Twilight unbuttons your overcoat.

            I feel a blush coming on.

I know the feeling.

            Just lay it on the line.

Easy for you to say.

            Speak for yourself.

Isn't that the problem?

            What are you sad about?

There once was a mother
and daughter.

            Come on, remember it like it was.

Okay. It was grand.
        That's a good start.

Grand, my mother
said and arched
the sky into
the canopy of her
mouth,
her newborn head
on my shoulder,
the razor shining
in its sleeve,
her hair buried
in the garden.

        Place your face here.

What if I tell
the wrong story?
        Place your face here.

Turning About in the Seat of Consciousness

I closed the book at Bloor & Yonge when I felt the
    crybaby
working up a crescendo in my throat.
Beside me sat a man who smelled of burnt toast and
    mortality
as the passengers got sucked out the doors
like astronauts in zero gravity.
From then on I was a passenger aboard the
    eastbound
train heading towards Tibet. *The Book of Living
and Dying* was at my fingertips, but a woman
kept looking at me with eyes that resembled
the eyes of a boy I loved in Hong Kong.
I tried to come up with a nice metaphor
for the colour of her hair but all I could think
of was motor oil. Not something pleasant like the
    night's
yin-dark soul. No, I was curled inside my small
ego trying to release thirty-three years of
    attachment,
my hands resting solemn as First Testaments
upon each knee – till the sun smashed its face
against the window like a pimple-faced teenager
and I found another metaphor
for breath.

The train railed to a stop above the parkway
and I saw what was once my life

standing on the bridge, waving her limp
handkerchief of defeat. The man beside me took
a deep breath and touched his forehead
with great formality, as if he had just delivered
a painful homily. I turned back to the figure
on the girder who introduced herself:

Renunciation, she said and extended her hand
through the window. I shook it with an enthusiasm
that scared her. She tried to let go,
but I held on.

Roll Call

It is a windy night.
The empty garbage bag
on the balcony scares me.
It is homeless as a thief.
It has shoulders that hunch
towards the window.
I place the book face-down.
See the picture of a man
who dug up the crowded
grave of Europe
and Russia. Searching
for the backbone
in the soul that continued
to rise in the death
camps. Day in
day out. From his chair
to the window to the top
of the stairs.
    Upon whose face
does the requiem begin?
There is a man with a beard
and point-blank reason. His eyes
carry wheelbarrows of night.
It is a hard darkness
that makes me place myself
on the cutting board. Gran's ring
on my finger reminds me to buck
up. It glistens a sterling
zero. Only thing left is downward
dog then bed. I walk to the window,

remind myself no one is watching
but the bag now filled with the body
of the wind. The clock has no idea
what time I'll fall asleep,
but I watch it as if it does.
The plant's leaves are giving
up their green. We try
but can't save her, can't
find the right mix of thirst
and water.
    Please call me.
The mouse appears out
of the corner of my eye, scurries
along the bookcase, curled bugle
cornchip in its mouth. Pauses on
Against Forgetting. Hears something.
Wriggles its cocky little
nose and shits on the pages.
The sound of a hand
against the window.
Don't be stupid. Just the bag
pressed against the glass. Stands
there, filthy. Crumples
back into itself. My heart
beats out a roll call. Everyone is missing.
    The mouse has gone back to
the behind-the-eyes world.
I pick up the book, place it
like a head in my lap.
    Compassion, he wrote,
means to suffer with, someone standing
by a river that admits everything,
someone lying beneath a neighbourhood
of clouds, someone waiting

at the top of the stairs. Ready to close
the distance. Dishevelled and torn,
the garbage bag slumps towards the edge
of the balcony. Shining down
the pale cheekbone
of the moon. Untouchable. Going
it alone. But for how long?
    I gather the pages of the book
between my finger and thumb,
release each one, press my face
to them. All the little unending
blows. Love, the only thing left
tonight is the rest –

Signs

All morning you smell the sweet oil
of bedsheets, moonwalk
away from every conversation, hear
french horn solos on little midnight
stages, unbutton
and button your shirt, long
for a briefcase with comforting
mechanical snaps. You can't
decide to be open
or shut, wonder where to hide
your confidentials. You worry
about the businessman,
feel stunned by the degradation
of his uncombed hair,
not at all hopeful
but wanting to hold
a teaspoon of a chance
to his lips.

* * *

Thursday leaks out the eye
of the squirrel hit by a car.
You watch the two-fisted
drag of its body across the road.
Pet the untamed bush
of its tail, touch the soft

scarf of fur, the lung's last
labour at 16:00 hours. Record
the nomenclature of a dead body
on the street. Clear a concrete
burial site of pop cans
and the rotten breath
of garbage. Make a place
for the animal to unzip
its one-piece suit and eye
a plane that jackhammers
the sky, ride a cloud to what might
be the other side.

* * *

Pink stargazers in the green pitcher
humiliate you. Vulvas open
as you sip from a white cup.
There are signs of the disappearing
woman: her crusted fingerprints
on the dead man's apron, her thin
reflection in the blade
of a butter knife. Stop talking
to ghosts in the upstairs closet.
Stop walking around limp
as a negligée. Catch all those words
dripping from the faucet.
Drink up. Let the flowers
lose their genitalia. Convince
yourself: nothing and no one
is as thirsty as
you think.

* * *

Meniscus of thought blurring Bloor,
Christie, Hallum. On the hour
every hour. Food finding its escape
route. The Norwegian bobsledders
in your gut. Nothing ever stays put.
Except this headache grunting
like a pig and the motherfucker parlance
and such particular endearments
to self. Lost in the wilderness voice.
You know the one. The one everyone
keeps waving to. Wanting turtlenecks
in 30 degrees, the oolong puddle
of autumn on your tongue,
children's voices as you pass
the park. Now you must become
the leaves, the teacher said
as their bodies curled
into themselves to worship
the tree.

* * *

That french horn on stage again.
You're solo at 4 a.m. Not even
the brief mercy of a bullet
to end this. Defenceless.
Needing the dark casket
of an hour, disembodied

from the moon. To place
the teaspoon in the drawer.
To read the news: see
the businessman in a bright
pylon-orange suit,
with the blindfold removed,
the nude look on his face
before the knife began
its crossing, before the voice
praised God, and severed
his head.

* * *

Where did that come from?

Little Black

The light on the river appears to be in the act
of remembering something important,

maybe some lifesaving parable it is teaching
the water and the water repeats it back to us.

You keep calling this denial but I'm waiting
for the sign that tells us where to place our feet.

Paramita means going

      to the other shore.

As sorrow's rowboat inches towards me
I place my feet upon the surface of the river.

* * *

We sit on the porch and my father wonders if next
    time
he might be the pine tree. I'm hoping to be a bird

or maybe the breeze that touches both feather and
    needle.
A family on two 4-wheelers drive by,

children clinging to adults like banners around

beauty-pageant queens. The loon takes aim at
the shoreline, cries its *come back* song that soars

like an arrow hitting the screen door of the past,
and the water reminds us that time is a proselytizer,

not a believer.

* * *

Outside I hear the rain's saintly surrender to shingle
and stone as my tongue homes in on the vowel

of your wilderness-tip. Little Black sleeps at the end

of the bed blowing a foghorn as you summon a song
through the eye of a needle.

Then the slow-motion flip into position
and you rest in the pond

of my spoon. Beneath the sheets our legs
play a violin of stubble and skin until sleep brings
   on

our separate lives.

* * *

Sunshine out there, leaves having a heyday,
gladiolas formalizing the view with their highbrow

gazes. There are ways in which I am fortunate:
this oak desk with the elbow stains that held the
    weight

of my grandmother's thinking, chocolate in my
    mouth,
Little Black on his pillow, Schubert climbing

a mountain,

                    ink in my pen.

Falling asleep last night I was thinking about guilt,
call it the square-shouldered matron of the family,

call it the girl hiding
under the stairs. Call it home for dinner with a
    steaming

plate of liver and onions.

* * *

Do you remember when we sat in the blue kitchen
till dawn, those wooden chairs creaking with blame
and self-deceit?
Unable to lie next to you I walked around
the neighbourhood as streetlamps lost their spot-lit
dramas, and the grey light of Sunday
morning anointed all my empty spaces.

Snowbanks ran up and down streets like
        linebackers.
I sat down on the shoulder of one and considered
leaving. But the thought felt like the angry god
of love tearing to pieces the pages of us till there

was nothing but piles and piles of winter.
Instead I carried home a paper bag of offerings,
lemon poppyseed your favourite, I mistook
my broken desire to please as an act
of generosity, and returned no different.

No different. With the thinker still finding fault in
        the heart
and the heart only wanting
to be wiser and the watcher hiding her
        disappointment
in the tight-eyed fists of red mitts.

* * *

The street lamp wears a fedora of light. Little Black
in the Colonel Mustard chair,

his limbs form the mystery of lock and key;
little one comfort me.
Out the window a man walks by with a mattress
on his head and a child

pushes an empty shopping cart. Hunger does its
    thunder
roll across the sky as Little Black

smacks his gums like an eighty-year-old before
the gravy boat, and I am smiling

like a garbageman on a sunny day with tears
    waiting
at the gates of not-now. I take a breath

    toward the heart, feel my lungs swell.
It's all changing – devotion and commitment

have taken a blood vessel

                    to the unknown.

* * *

Little Black flash me that wanton-smile and carry
your body, that wartime house,
                            across the river.

I was outside the Four Seasons, watching the black-
    gloved hands
of autumn direct ticket holders into *War and Peace*.
Every now and then the requiem of falling
leaves, wool coats moving like horses down
    darkened

streets. And then she appeared: the woman with
    grey hair,

her purple scarf performing a small flamenco,
noose of fabric, the wind, the decade that passed

as I sat there getting ready to cross four lanes of
    traffic
and start living for the sake of impulse,

not return, to recognize my longing in the body of a
    stranger
as she disappeared into the production

of someone else's life.

That was the night before Little Black
died, took the shadow-train underground
beneath October's dream of tulips.

* * *

Every room in the house has a pulse that draws me
in. I stand in the back room, stare out the window

trying to find its source, as if silence has taken her
    finger,
licked it, and plays all the open mouths

of wineglasses.

* * *

Little Black took the apple from my hand,
changed the tune of floorboards at 6 a.m.

and the song of passion without reason as it passed
    through
the throat of an abandoned dog from Michigan.

* * *

If knowing is a sharp, shiny instrument and feeling
is a serrated edge then surrender must

be the hand that holds everything.

* * *

Little Black turned love into a top-hat magic-trick,
a warm animal pulled from the human's
                                        blackhole.

* * *

Last night I dreamt my mother was staring
at a painting. Above her a slab

of dusk descended into a field of poppies
standing proud as dead
soldiers in the memory of widows.

She turned towards me to deliver the one line
I've never heard.

Curving her arms into half-moons,
her face sitting between them like a Goddess
from a myth that had no storyteller, she said,

Give this to your father because I'm glad
he was in my life.

Just like that,
before she turned and placed her face
in the field again.

* * *

Sometimes I listen to the world so closely
I can feel what it is saying

in my crotch, especially on park benches
when humans are banking their hours and it's just
    me

and the birds who strut their Saturday night fevers
toward breadcrumbs that shine like 14 karat

flecks of gold in the dead grass.

* * *

Little Black thought it was a good idea to follow
the blonde with bad roots

everywhere, and he was right.
He was always right.

* * *

The day I moved you decided to stay home,
helped me carry the beer boxes with a heavy metal

mover named Mike who became Atlas – balancing
    my world on his back.

And it was impossible to say just how hopeful
the watcher was – standing there in the snow,

her red mittens clapping to get the circulation of
    touch
merrily rushing back into a vision

even the heart could see.

* * *

Little Black no longer at his post
by the fridge door, no burst down the hardwood

runway, no toenails singing in the rain, no sidewalk
to jackhandy his flip-flop walk,

no more no more *mon amour* no more.

* * *

This year I discovered *paramita* in the waters of that
   one

   man who loved so deeply he married the river

Darest thou now O soul
               he married the farmboy's fagotry
Walk out with me toward the unknown

               he married the moon's blind eye

Where neither ground is for the feet

he married words to the wind horse

nor any path to follow
                       to the lies and the gossip and
   the truth of the river

as it pours out the mouth of right-now

* * *

I made you a set of keys for the light inside
this room as it chastises

the scrapyard solitude I can't live
without. Beyond the window shines spraycan

graffiti that sticks it to the man. Right now
I wouldn't trade regret

or apology for the beaten down
path of entitlement. You are not mine

and I am not yours, which means I love you
with the heart
                of a coureur de bois.

* * *

These mornings I wake to the 35 mm roll
of trains heading towards the lake.

Four stories above the treetops I watch
with the red-winged blackbirds as the sun crowns

the raw material of the city and the clouds
hang their hats on high-rises and the heavens

keep performing the longest running
peepshow on earth.

And eventually – once the teacup is filled
and emptied, once the apple is admired,

once the floorboards have woken and settle
into their key of absence – I enter the day,

let the water have its way with me.

I climb into my boat, heave-ho,
and row

        the unstoppable row

with the soft pads of a song pawing
up my throat, an imperfect praise to sadness,

an embarrassing ode to old joy,
the goodbye-you're-gone-hello-we-keep-on,
the song I learned from Little Black.

October

When that scrap of velvet died in our arms it was
    unlike
any sorrow I carried.
Grief was exactly 21.2 pounds of flesh and fur.

Death drew up his eyelids to reveal the iris
slowly closing
              like the last door

in the last room where we buried him with his
    blanket
and Empire Apple; we were burying that part of us
           that died too. We took turns digging
and when the hole was deep enough we climbed in.

          I hated this season,
hated the stain the birds were leaving
in the trees, hated the elderly sweep of leaves,
hated being left behind with only his scent and
    shape
         on my hands.

He was devotion in a clown's suit, he was
    heartbreak on
a lifelong bender, he was the knuckle-bone of trust,
and for a time, he was the sum of us. We covered
    him
with dirt and when there was no hole left to cover,

the shovel hit the ground like a body and we curled
    around
the sound loss makes above the earth.

                        One year later your cold-lipped
October kiss still makes my blood surge, asking
    questions like,
Do the dead lie
                        next to the unborn?
And if so, what do they talk about? I can't make
    heads or tails
of my doubt, my morality,

my cross-legged compass. But the proof is in the
    pudding-faced
ghost and you are the constant return my heart

loops and loops like a dog rounding the fenced-in
yard of his home.

Here are my failures that did not die with him,
though I wish they had. I'll lay them out for you
like the neatly pressed suit I climbed into today
when I sat down to write you.

Notes and Acknowledgements

"Sibling of the Air" is for Newt.

"Fear of Death Confounds Me" was written after reading *Otherwise* by Jane Kenyon (Graywolf Press: 1996), "timor mortis conturbat me" discovered in Donald Hall's *Without* (Mariner Books: 1998).

The title "Take Notes" and "take notes, and the pain goes" are from Virginia Woolf's *The Years* (Penguin: 1998).

"The Move" is for Suzanne.

"A Conversation With Horizon" Lines 6, 18, 24, & 97 are from Phyllis Webb's poem "Some Final Questions" in *Selected Poems 1954-1965* (Talonbooks: 1971); also inspired by the Rocky Mountains and a lecture given by the writer Reza Baraheni.

"Goodness" is for Wheeza, Aunt Cheri, Mary Jane, and Roxana. Written in memory of Betsy Balderston and Carol Shields.

"Roll Call" was written in memory of Terence Des Pres, after reading his book *The Survivor: An Anatomy of Life in the Death Camps* (Oxford University Press: 1976).

"Little Black" is for Evalyn. "Paramita means going to the other shore" is from Pema Chödrön's *When Things Fall Apart* (Shambhala Publications: 1997). Walt Whitman's "Darest thou now O soul walk out with me to the unknown... where neither ground is for the feet nor any path to follow" is from *Leaves of Grass* (Signet Classic: 2000).

"October" was written in memory of Amos, a.k.a. Little Black.

Versions of these poems have appeared in *Existere, THIS Magazine, The Fiddlehead,* and *Third Floor Lounge: An Anthology of Poetry from the Banff Centre for the Arts Writing Studio 2004* (little-fishcartpress, 2004).

My appreciation to the editors. I am grateful to the Ontario Arts Council for their financial support, to the participants and faculty of the Banff Centre for the Arts Writer's Studio of 2004, and the Canada Council for the Arts travel grant.

As well my thanks to Pete Doherty, Ronna Bloom, Dave Cameron, Brad Hart, Harry Howie, Sarah Goodman, Kate

Huband, Anna Chatteron, Karin Randoja. Thanks to Soraya Peerbaye for her poet-self, asking all the important questions. And to Abby Hershler for her steadfast heart, always making a place for me in the attic.

Unending thanks to Suzanne Hancock for providing such wisdom to my writing and love to my life.

Gratitude to my family: Marilynn, Dave, Peter, Cate, Stephanie, Hector, Kai, Skylar, Rosemary, Caroline, Richard, and the Robertson and Toombs clans. And to Dylan, Lara, Harvey, and Johanna.

Deepest thanks and love to my partner, Evalyn Parry; astute, devoted reader, every poet needs a Peggy Wingbat.

And finally, enormous thanks to my editor Elana Wolff for her belief, insight and guidance; and to Michael Mirolla, Connie McParland and Antonio D'Alfonso at Guernica Editions.

"Suzanne Robertson's début collection of poetry is a glimpse into the mesmerizing psyche and sensibility of a person whose poetic ear and eye are always close to the ground. The narrator of these poems 'listen[s] to the world so closely,' that the most tangential and ordinary moments are somehow transformed into such startling beauty as 'the rustle of two cats falling / In love.' Yet the observing eye is always respectful, offering up image after image that resonates with intelligence and craft. Robertson takes us on an inward and thought-provoking journey that leads to the achingly beautiful elegy for 'Little Black.' This is a book whose depth and power lie in Robertson's questioning of what it means to be a fully sentient human." — Laura Lush

In her first collection of poems, Suzanne Robertson meditates on the nature of intimacy; the connective tissue that binds stranger to stranger, human to animal, soul to landscape, heart to mind. Inspired by the Buddhist paramitas – actions that spark a spiritual sojourn, the poems attempt to both transcend and stay grounded in a conventional universe. Follow the humourous, pedestrian plight of a secretary/writer grappling with her noonday demon, her love affair with Little Black, and the metamorphosis of her marriage as she harnesses the practical power of poetry, marrying words "to the wind horse," "to the lies and the gossip and the truth of the river / as it pours out the mouth of right now." Paramita, Little Black explores acts of transformation; documenting a journey to live and love authentically amidst the transient anatomy of our twenty-first century lives.

A Toronto writer and photographer, Suzanne Robertson works at the Children's Aid Society, is a member of PEN Canada and Gallery 44 Centre for Contemporary Photography, and volunteers with Hospice Toronto.

Printed in March 2011
by Gauvin Press,
Gatineau, Québec